FOOD WEBS

GRASSLAND

Food Webs

By William Anthony

BookLife PUBLISHING

©2019
BookLife Publishing Ltd.
King's Lynn
Norfolk PE30 4LS

All rights reserved.
Printed in Malaysia.

A catalogue record for this book is available from the British Library.

ISBN: 978-1-78637-622-0

Written by:
William Anthony

Edited by:
Kirsty Holmes

Designed by:
Jasmine Pointer

All facts, statistics, web addresses and URLs in this book were verified as valid and accurate at time of writing. No responsibility for any changes to external websites or references can be accepted by either the author or publisher.

Photocredits:
Images are courtesy of Shutterstock.com. With thanks to Getty Images, Thinkstock Photo and iStockphoto.

aradaphotography (earth texture), YamabikaY (paper texture). Front cover - Ian Rentoul, Patthana Nirangkul, Kanea, Leo Blanchette. 2 – Volodymyr Burdiak. 3 – nuruddean. 4&5 – JaySi. 6 – Edmund O'Connor, Black Sheep Media, Dirk M. de Boer. 7 – markusmayer, Benny Marty, PHOTOCREO Michal Bednarek. 6 & 7 – aodaodaodaod. 8 – SAROJ GURJAR. 9 – EcoPrint, ArCaLu, John Michael Vosloo, Eric Isselee. 10 – Stuart G Porter. 11 – Svetography, Stacey Ann Alberts, NaturesMomentsuk, Bob Pool. 12 – Beate Wolter, Edmund O'Connor, Black Sheep Media. 13 – Eric Isselee, Dr Ajay Kumar Singh, Pavel Krasensky. 14 – EcoPrint. 15 – Ana Gram, Edwin Godinho, Succulent, nwdph. 16 – Carlos A Antunes, Simon Eeman. 17 – Simon Eeman, Johan Swanepoel. 18 – Ondrej Prosicky. 19 – Eric Isselee, Stuart G Porter, Nicola Destefano. 20 – PACO COMO. 21 – Eric Isselee, E X P L O R E R. 23 – Thomas Retterath.

CONTENTS

Page 4   In the Grasslands
Page 6   The Food Web
Page 8   The Lion
Page 10 The Caracal
Page 12 The Mouse
Page 14 The Hare
Page 16 The Eagle
Page 18 The Striped Hyena
Page 20 The Cheetah
Page 22 Grassland Food Web
Page 24 Glossary and Index

Words that look like THIS can be found in the glossary on page 24.

IN THE GRASSLANDS

Go on a safari, see the wonderful sights... but be careful! Do you know who might be sneaking through the tall grass, looking for a meal?

There are lots of different animals and plants to be found, all going about their daily business, and each and every one of them has a place in the food web.

Let's look at who-eats-who in the grasslands. Who can we find in the African SAVANNAH...

THE FOOD WEB

...It all starts with the Sun's energy...

...which feeds plants...

...HERBIVORES eat the plants...

...**CARNIVORES** eat the herbivores...

...bigger **PREDATORS** eat them...

...and **APEX PREDATORS** eat those.

THE LION

Keep your distance – I'm a lion and I'm an apex predator here in the African savannah. That means I never have to look out for someone wanting to eat me because I'm too big and strong! It also means I have lots of PREY to choose from for my dinner...

NAME:	Lion
TYPE:	MAMMAL
HOME:	Africa
FOOD:	Carnivore
PREDATOR OR PREY?:	Apex Predator

8

Hare: small but a great snack...?

Wildebeest: strong but a big feast...?

Thomson's gazelle: quick but delicious...?

I'm bored of eating the same old things. I want a special treat. What's that over there in the grass? It looks tasty...

QUICK, TURN THE PAGE!

THE CARACAL

I'm a caracal and I really don't want to mess with that lion. We are both a type of cat, but lions are one of the biggest cats in the world! If I can stay out of sight, I can get on with finding my own food.

NAME:	Caracal
TYPE:	Mammal
HOME:	Africa and Asia
FOOD:	Carnivore
PREDATOR OR PREY?:	Both

Mongoose: furry but definitely not friendly...?

Hare: jumpy but juicy...?

Thomson's gazelle: big but brilliant...?

All that worry about the lion has made me lose my appetite. Well, maybe I could just have a small snack instead...

WHO'S THE SNACK?

THE MOUSE

I may be snack-sized for all the animals that want to eat me, but that also means I'm harder for them to spot! Besides, I've got to worry about a different type of animal when it comes to food...

NAME:	Mouse
TYPE:	Mammal
HOME:	All Over the World
FOOD:	Herbivore
PREDATOR OR PREY?:	Prey

12

I have to compete with the other herbivores for my food. I love eating different types of grass, but so do these animals:

Hare: a furry issue...

Harvester ant: a nippy nuisance...

Topi: a horned problem...

IS THAT A HARE?

13

THE HARE

Us herbivores all have to share. We can't afford to spend time fighting over food while there are lots of predators on our tails! I'm a hare and I have a lot of big animals after me for their dinner...

NAME:	Hare
TYPE:	Mammal
HOME:	Africa, North America, Europe and Asia
FOOD:	Herbivore
PREDATOR OR PREY?:	Prey

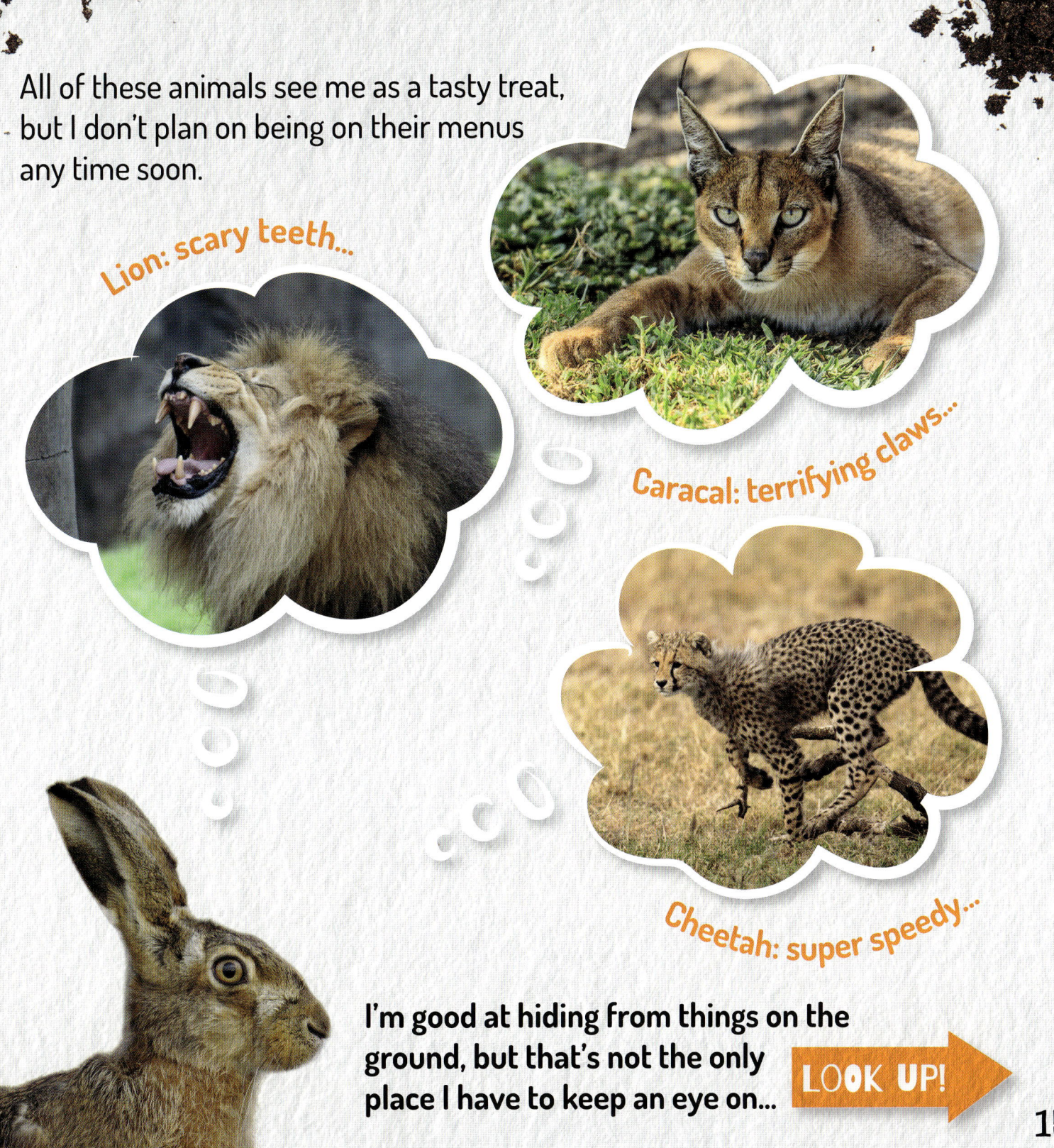

All of these animals see me as a tasty treat, but I don't plan on being on their menus any time soon.

Lion: scary teeth...

Caracal: terrifying claws...

Cheetah: super speedy...

I'm good at hiding from things on the ground, but that's not the only place I have to keep an eye on...

LOOK UP!

15

THE EAGLE

No! The hare spotted me! I was so close to a tasty treat. I'm an eagle and I can soar through the skies to spot my breakfast, lunch and dinner from above.

NAME:	Eagle
TYPE:	Bird
HOME:	All Over the World
FOOD:	Carnivore
PREDATOR OR PREY?:	Apex Predator

I'm an apex predator in these grasslands and I'll eat anything! What do I fancy today?

Mouse: a tiny treat...?

Wildebeest: some lovely leftovers...?

Hare: a hopping feast...?

I'm so tired today – I'm going to SCAVENGE some of the lion's wildebeest leftovers rather than catch my own dinner.

WAIT, WHO'S THAT?

17

THE STRIPED HYENA

That eagle has got the right idea! I'm a striped hyena and I'm a scavenger. Why would you waste time and effort to catch your own dinner when you can just steal someone else's?

NAME:	Striped Hyena
TYPE:	Mammal
HOME:	Africa
FOOD:	OMNIVORE
PREDATOR OR PREY?:	Apex Predator

As I keep myself to myself, nothing much likes to eat me, so I'm also an apex predator. I'm licking my lips at the look of today's menu...

Caracal: the lion's spares...?

Aardvark: the lioness's leavings...?

Topi: the lion's leftovers...?

Wildebeest: the cheetah's scraps...?

TURN THE PAGE... BUT QUIETLY...!

19

THE CHEETAH

Psst! Be quiet and don't alert my prey. Had you forgotten about me? Good – that's exactly what I wanted. I'm a cheetah and I hunt silently until I'm ready to pounce. I can see three of my favourite meals, but which should I go for?

NAME:	Cheetah
TYPE:	Mammal
HOME:	Africa
FOOD:	Carnivore
PREDATOR OR PREY?:	Apex Predator

Wildebeest: delicious but big and strong...?

Hare: tasty but not very filling...?

Thomson's gazelle: yummy but hard to catch...?

I'm going for the gazelle. They're very fast, but I'm the fastest land animal in the world – and I do like a challenge...

GRASSLAND FOOD WEB

The arrows follow where the energy goes. Can you follow the energy from the Sun all the way to the apex predators?

HYENA

EAGLE

MONGOOSE

LION

CHEETAH

CARACAL

AARDVARK

HARE

HARVESTER ANTS

THOMSON'S GAZELLE

MOUSE

GRASS

WILDEBEEST

TOPI

PRODUCER	CONSUMER	APEX PREDATOR
Makes their own food using energy from the Sun.	Eats producers, or other consumers.	Nothing eats these.

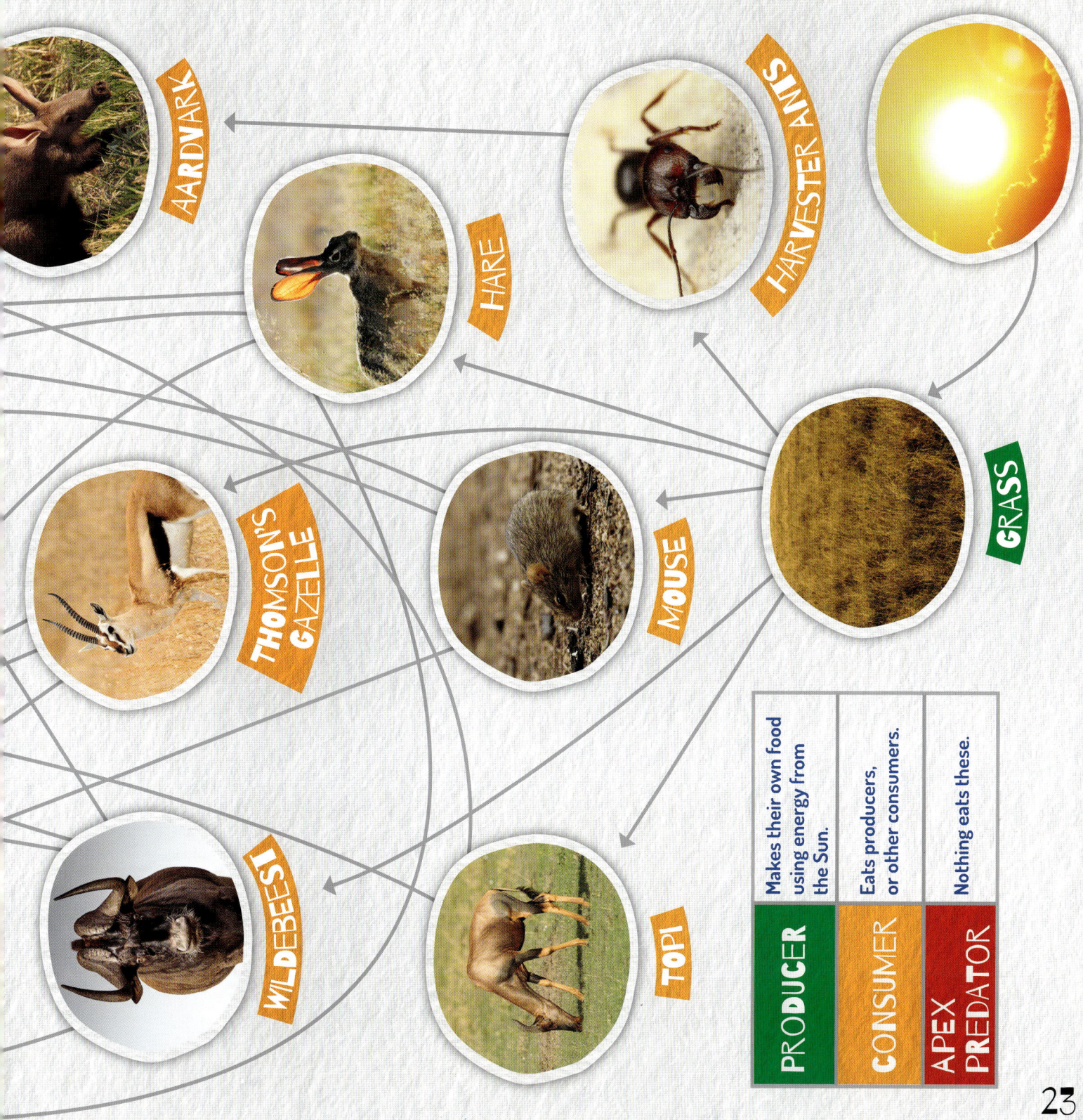

23

GLOSSARY

apex predators	the top predators in a food chain, with no natural predators of their own
carnivores	animals that eat other animals, instead of plants
herbivores	animals that eat plants, instead of other animals
mammal	an animal that has warm blood, a backbone and produces milk
omnivore	an animal that eats both plants and other animals
predators	animals that hunt other animals for food
prey	animals that are hunted for food
savannah	a large area of flat land with grass and very few trees
scavenge	to feed on other animals that are already dead

INDEX

apex predators 7–8, 16–20, 22–23
Africa 5–6, 10, 14, 18, 20
Asia 10, 14
birds 16
carnivores 7–8, 10, 16, 20
energy 6, 22–23
Europe 14
herbivores 6–7, 12–14
mammals 8, 10, 12, 14, 18, 20
North America 14
scavengers 16–19